Brian Urlacher

by Michael Sandler

Consultant: Norries Wilson
Head Football Coach, Columbia University

BEARPORT
PUBLISHING

New York, New York

Credits

Cover, © Jonathan Daniel/Getty Images; Title Page, © Scott Boehm/Getty Images; 4, © Paul Jasienski/Getty Images; 5, © Ross D. Franklin/Reuters/Landov; 6, © AP Images/Rick Hossman; 7, © Scott Boehm/Getty Images; 9, © AP Images/Jake Schoellkopf; 10, © AP Images/Albuquerque Journal/Jim Thompson; 11, © AP Images/Jake Schoellkopf; 12, © Tony Tomsic/NFL/Getty Images; 13, © Frank Polich/UPI/Landov; 14, © Jonathan Daniel/Getty Images; 15, © Brian Bahr/Getty Images; 16, Courtesy of the Chicago Bears; 17, © AP Photo/Enid News & Eagle/Kyle Nosal; 18, © AP Images/Jake Schoellkopf; 19, © AP Images/Albuquerque Journal/Jim Thompson; 20, Courtesy of the Chicago Bears; 21, Courtesy of the Chicago Bears; 22, © Scott Boehm/Getty Images; 22Logo, © KRT/Newscom.

Publisher: Kenn Goin
Senior Editor: Lisa Wiseman
Creative Director: Spencer Brinker
Photo Researcher: Omni-Photo Communications, Inc.
Design: Dawn Beard Creative

Library of Congress Cataloging-in-Publication Data

Sandler, Michael, 1965–
  Brian Urlacher / by Michael Sandler.
      p. cm. — (Football heroes making a difference)
  Includes bibliographical references and index.
  ISBN-13: 978-1-59716-775-8 (library binding)
  ISBN-10: 1-59716-775-4 (library binding)
  1. Urlacher, Brian—Juvenile literature. 2. Football players—United States—Biography—Juvenile literature. 3. Football players—United States—Conduct of life—Juvenile literature. I. Title.
  GV939.U76S36 2009
  796.332092—dc22
  [B]
                                 2008034878

For more information, write to Bearport Publishing Company, Inc., 45 West 21st Street, Suite 3B, New York, NY 10010. Printed in the United States of America in North Mankato, Minnesota.

082010
080910CGC

10 9 8 7 6 5 4 3

CONTENTS

No Time to Lose

For the first five weeks of the 2006 season, the Chicago Bears couldn't lose. Their winning streak had fans dreaming of the Super Bowl.

However, Chicago's sixth game on October 16, 2006, was turning into a nightmare. They were losing, 23-3, to the Arizona Cardinals. With just a quarter left to play, Chicago's winning streak seemed close to an end.

Brian Urlacher, the Bears' big **linebacker**, wasn't happy about it. *This team is too good to lose like this*, he thought. Could one player make a difference and bring the team back? Brian was going to try.

Brian watches his team from the sidelines during the game on October 16, 2006.

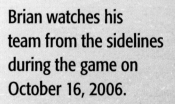

4

Brian (#54) unsuccessfully tries to tackle Arizona Cardinals receiver Anquan Boldin (#81).

Catching Up

Brian took over the game. He **rushed** the Cardinals' quarterback. He made tackle after tackle. Soon his teammates followed his lead, turning a Cardinals **fumble** into a Chicago touchdown. The score was now 23-10.

Next, Brian ripped the ball loose from Arizona's Edgerrin James. Brian's teammate Charles Tillman scooped it up. He zoomed 40 yards (37 m) for another touchdown. Now it was 23-17.

Then, the Bears' defense forced Arizona to **punt**. Chicago's Devin Hester caught the ball and ran all the way into the **end zone**. Touchdown! Brian and the Bears had an amazing 24-23 win.

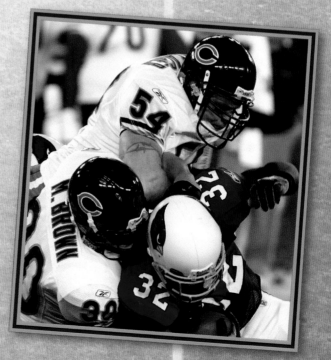

Brian (#54) and his teammate Mike Brown (#30) tackle Arizona's running back Edgerrin James (#32).

During their 20-point comeback, the Bears' defense and **special teams** scored all the touchdowns—an NFL first!

A Skinny Kid

No one ever expected Brian Urlacher to become an NFL star. Growing up in New Mexico, he was so skinny that his friends called him a "scrawny pipsqueak."

Small or not, Brian loved sports. He worked hard to become a better athlete. In high school, he told his coach to yell at him more often. "It makes me play harder," said Brian.

Brian also spent hundreds of hours in the weight room trying to make himself strong enough for football. In two years, Brian gained 60 pounds (27 kg) of muscle. He soon became the best player on his high school team. In fact, Brian became the best high school player in the state.

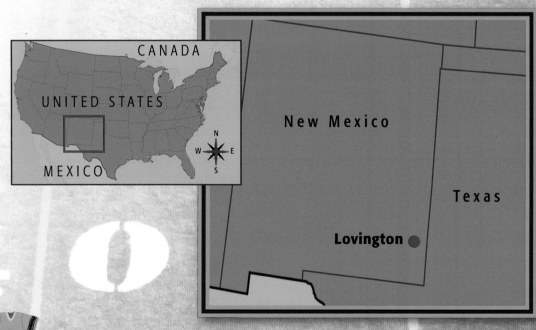

Brian grew up in Lovington, New Mexico.

This is the football field that Brian played on while attending Lovington High School.

In his senior year, Brian's high school football team went 14-0. They were the New Mexico state champions.

College Star

During high school, Brian played two positions, wide receiver on **offense** and **safety** on defense. Then in college, at the University of New Mexico, the coach began playing him as a linebacker, too. Brian did very well in his new position. "Every game," remembers his coach, "Brian did something that made you say, 'wow!'"

NFL **scouts** said "wow" as well—especially scouts from Chicago. The Bears chose Brian with the ninth pick in the 2000 NFL **draft**.

Brian during football practice at the University of New Mexico

Brian (#44) charges downfield during a game against Colorado State University on November 6, 1999.

At the University of New Mexico, Brian was an **All-American** on defense and caught six touchdown passes as a wide receiver.

First Season

The jump from college to the NFL wasn't easy for Brian. He played poorly at first. "It was frustrating," he remembers.

By midseason, however, he got his game together. His speed and strength helped him make tackles and **sack** quarterbacks. Pretty soon, people compared him to Hall of Fame Bears linebackers such as Mike Singletary and Dick Butkus.

All that was missing for Brian was winning. The Bears finished 5-11 in his **rookie year**. Chicago needed more than tackles and sacks. The team needed a leader.

Dick Butkus played for the Chicago Bears from 1965–1973.

Brian (#54) makes a tackle during his rookie year in 2000.

After the 2000 season, Brian was named NFL Defensive Rookie of the Year. He also made the **Pro Bowl**.

Taking Charge

Brian decided to become the leader that the Bears needed. He demanded results—from himself and the team. "When he messes up, he owns up to it. When you mess up, he jumps down your throat. That's why he's our leader," said teammate Alex Brown.

With Brian taking charge, the Bears began to win. They made the playoffs in 2001, and again in 2005. Then, in 2006, Chicago started the season with a seven-game winning streak. They played well all season and finally reached Super Bowl XLI (41) to play the Indianapolis Colts.

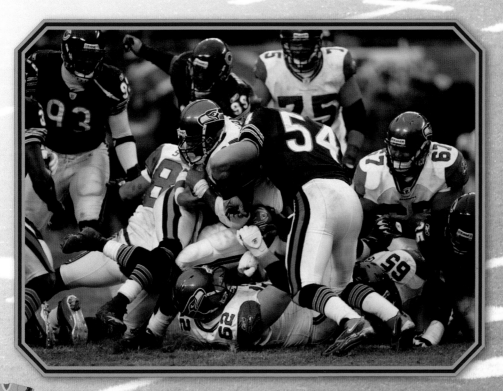

The Bears during a playoff game after the 2006 season

Brian (#54), some of his teammates, and players from the Colts during the coin toss before Super Bowl XLI (41)

URLACHER
54

KREUTZ
57

MANNELLY
65

MUHAMMAD
87

58

4

18

LJ
101

FJ
82

LJ
10

Super Bowl XLI (41) was Chicago's first trip to the big game since 1986.

Helping Special Kids

Brian had made a difference for his team. Now he wanted to make a difference off the field—by improving the lives of children. One way he does this is by working with the Special Olympics. This group helps children with **intellectual disabilities** develop self-confidence through playing sports. It gives them training and holds competitions.

Brian gives both money and time to the organization. Each year, he invites a lucky group of kids to meet and spend time with him at the Bears' **training camp**. Once he even went on the TV game show *Wheel of Fortune*. He won $47,000, splitting the money between the Special Olympics groups in Illinois and New Mexico.

Brian (back row, third from left) spends time with some kids from the Special Olympics after a Bears home game in 2007.

A 50-meter (54-yard) race held during a 2006 Special Olympics event in Enid, Oklahoma

Every year, Brian buys a block of season tickets—33 in 2008—to each Bears home game. He gives them out to children from the Special Olympics.

High School Help

Even after he became a football star in Chicago, Brian never forgot his hometown high school. Lovington High School had helped get him to the NFL, so Brian wanted to help Lovington High.

In 2002, he **donated** $40,000 to improve the weight room where he had grown from a scrawny kid into a powerful athlete. He also paid for better locker rooms in the gym. Brian is "one of the kindest human beings I've ever met," said high school football coach Jaime Quinones. "He has never forgotten his roots."

The new weight room at Lovington High School

In 2001, Brian's high school football jersey was retired.

One year, Brian even paid for some students from Lovington High to go on a senior trip to Lubbock, Texas.

Always Keep Trying

Brian's NFL career has had moments of greatness and moments of pain. On the very first play of Super Bowl XLI (41), Brian took the lead as always. He reached up to knock down an Indianapolis pass, causing an **incompletion**. Yet later, he felt the sting of losing. The Colts won the Super Bowl, defeating Chicago, 29-17.

Brian will never stop trying to lead Chicago to a Super Bowl title. He will also never stop trying to make a difference in the lives of kids. Winning is important, but helping to change lives matters even more.

Brian often visits schools and works with students to help teach them the importance of physical fitness.

Brian enjoys the time he spends with his young fans.

Brian has been voted to the Pro Bowl six times in his career.

The Brian File

Brian is a football hero on and off the field. Here are some highlights.

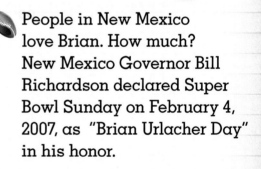

- Each summer, Brian runs a football camp. Hundreds of kids practice real NFL drills and get to meet and spend time with Brian.

- In his career with the Bears, Brian has made over 900 tackles.

- Many NFL defenders dance around and celebrate after making a tackle, except for Brian. After he knocks a player down, Brian helps him back up. To him, it's just good sportsmanship.

- People in New Mexico love Brian. How much? New Mexico Governor Bill Richardson declared Super Bowl Sunday on February 4, 2007, as "Brian Urlacher Day" in his honor.

- In Lovington, Brian holds a yearly charity basketball game. Brian and other NFL players play hoops and raise money for the high school's athletic program.

 Glossary

All-American (AWL-uh-MER-uh-kuhn) a high school or college player who is named one of the best at his position in the entire country

defensive (di-FEN-siv) responsible for stopping the other team from scoring

donated (DOH-nate-id) gave something as a gift

draft (DRAFT) an event in which professional teams take turns choosing college athletes to play for them

end zone (END ZOHN) the area at either end of a football field where touchdowns are scored

fumble (FUHM-buhl) a ball dropped or lost by the player who had it

incompletion (*in*-kuhm-PLEE-shuhn) a pass that is thrown, but not caught

intellectual disabilities (in-tuh-LEK-choo-uhl *diss*-uh-BIL-uh-teez) difficulties with thinking, remembering, or learning

linebacker (LINE-bak-ur) a defensive player on the second line who makes tackles and defends passes

offense (AW-fenss) the players on a football team whose job it is to score points

Pro Bowl (PROH BOHL) the yearly all-star game for the season's best NFL players

punt (PUHNT) a kick in which a specific player drops the ball and kicks it before it hits the ground

rookie year (RUK-ee YIRH) the first year that an athlete plays on a team

rushed (RUSHT) tried to get at the other team's quarterback in order to tackle him or stop him from passing

sack (SAK) to tackle a quarterback behind the line of scrimmage while he's attempting to throw a pass

safety (SAYF-tee) a defensive player who lines up farther back than other defensive players

scouts (SKOUTS) people who search for talented young athletes to play on teams

special teams (SPESH-uhl TEEMZ) a group of players who come onto the field only at specific times such as kickoffs, field goal attempts, and punts

training camp (TRAYN-ing KAMP) the place where NFL players practice for several weeks as they get ready for a new season

Bibliography

Brown, Clifton. "A Position of Greatness, and a Hunger for Victory." *The New York Times* (January 14, 2007).

Korte, Tim. "Urlacher Keeps Close to His Roots." *Associated Press* (February 4, 2007).

www.chicagobears.com

www.urlacherfootball.com

Read More

Sandler, Michael. *Peyton Manning and the Indianapolis Colts: Super Bowl XLI.* New York: Bearport Publishing (2008).

Stewart, Mark. *The Chicago Bears.* Chicago, IL: Norwood House Press (2007).

Uschan, Michael V. *Brian Urlacher.* Broomall, PA: Maso Crest (2008).

Learn More Online

To learn more about Brian Urlacher and the Chicago Bears, visit
www.bearportpublishing.com/FootballHeroes

Index